Red Wing Stoneware

By
Dan DePasquale
Gail DePasquale
Larry Peterson

COLLECTOR BOOKS
P.O. Box 3009
Paducah, KY 42001

The current values in this book should be used only as a guide. They are not intended to set prices, which vary from one section of the country to another. Auction prices as well as dealer prices vary greatly and are affected by condition as well as demand. Neither the Authors nor the Publisher assumes responsibility for any losses that might be incurred as a result of consulting this guide.

Acknowledgments

No book of this nature can ever be published without the help and support of others. We would like to recognize Gary and Bonnie Tefft for their assistance and for their permission to use selected photos from their book *Red Wing Potters and Their Wares*. Also, a special "Thank you" goes to Ray Pahnke for sending photos from the Chicago area and to Lyndon Viel for sharing additional pictures with us.

Others gave support, shared expertise and/or allowed us to photograph their collections. To them, we are truly grateful.

Illinois
  Dave and Kathy Kuffel
  Ray and Nadine Pahnke
  Taugie and Beth Slaith
Iowa
  Dan and Jo Allers
  Larry and Pat Ambler
  George and Rosie Boggess
  Dick and Elaine Fastenau
  Nancy Johnson
  Richard and Frances Larsen
  Phil Warren
Kansas
  Richard Cronemeyer
  Don and Eleanor Denney
  Ron and Marilyn Richardson
  Willard Wiley
Minnesota
  Susan Gilmer
  Evelyn Mayer
  Rachel Morris
  Jim Norine

Jewell Peterson
  Gordon and Pat Ray
  Jack and Mary Lou Valek
Missouri
  Cecil and Pat Aulgur
  Henry Heflin
  Dean Johnson
Nebraska
  Duane and Nan Baker
  Dr. Charles and Georgia
    Hales
  Pat and Mary McGilvrey
  Lonnie and Donna Spies
  Leo and Susie Schotte
Wisconsin
  Ed Herman
  Craig McNab
  Gary and Bonnie Tefft
  Lyndon Viel

The Goodhue County Historical Society
The Red Wing Pottery Salesroom

History of the Stoneware Companies of Red Wing, Minnesota

The stoneware industry came to Red Wing because the right conditions existed. Glaciers had deposited perfect clay in the area, there were capital and manpower in the town, and there was a functional need for the product at that time in history.

It was only when the Red Wing Stoneware Company began producing stoneware on a large scale in 1878 that the product became known beyond the local area. Due to this initial success, a new company, The Minnesota Stoneware Company, was formed in 1883. Both companies prospered, expanded the number of products manufactured and made capital improvements to their respective plants. In 1892 still another stoneware company was formed--the North Star Stoneware Company. Economic conditions were not favorable for expansion and growth during this period; hence, all three companies suffered.

In an effort to weather the economic difficulties, the three companies formed a single selling consortium, the Union Stoneware Company. The "Union" was to cut competition among the three companies by serving as a clearing house that "farmed out" stoneware orders to the three companies. While the Red Wing and Minnesota Companies were able to ride out the poor economic conditions, the North Star Company faltered. In 1896 the North Star Company ceased production and its share of the "Union" was bought out by the other two companies.

Conditions improved with the introduction of white ware in the late 1890's. The two remaining Red Wing stoneware companies totally combined in March 1906 to form the Red Wing Union Stoneware Company. This action was prompted, perhaps, as a means to meet the threat of the newly formed Western Stoneware Company in Illinois.

In 1936, the company name was changed to Red Wing Potteries. After a long union strike, the Potteries was closed in 1967--thus ending a long and proud tradition.

Table of Contents

Introduction

For many years now, decorated stoneware made in the eastern United States has been highly prized by collectors. Interest in it has, in fact, caused it to be synonomous with the word "stoneware" in general. A look at almost any published antique price guide will verify this misconception.

Midwesterners who, in the past, preferred stoneware products which were manufactured in their own region were thought to have inferior taste. It has only been in the last five or six years that collectors of midwestern stoneware, in general, and of stoneware produced in Red Wing, Minnesota, specifically, have begun to take pride in their collecting and to share with others of similar interests knowledge of Red Wing products. Consequently, Red Wing stoneware collecting has seen a remarkable and exciting growth which, even now, has grown beyond the Midwest and has become nation-wide in its appeal.

The uniqueness and the variety of pieces which were manufactured in Red Wing during the companies' ninety year history provide something for everybody--no matter what their interest or how big or how small their pocketbook. It would be impossible in a book of any size, to illustrate and/or describe every piece ever produced. In addition, previously unknown pieces are constantly being uncovered--adding new excitement to an already expanding hobby. The fun is in the finding and the sharing and in the meeting of others who enthusiastically pursue this mutual obsession.

Summary of Red Wing, Minnesota Stoneware Companies

1. Red Wing Stoneware Company--1877-1906
2. Minnesota Stoneware Company--1883-1906
3. North Star Stoneware Company--1892-1896
4. Union Stoneware Company--1894-1906
5. Red Wing Union Stoneware Company--1906-1936
6. Red Wing Potteries--1936-1967

CHAPTER I: Why Collect?

Many of the same factors that encouraged the collecting of eastern stoneware in the past have contributed to the popularity of Red Wing collecting today. i.e. beauty, affordability, uniqueness in function and design, and investment opportunities in these inflationary times. The appeal for collectors of Red Wing products, however, transcends even these obvious reasons.

It seems that four main reasons stand out above all others. One, there is a growing interest in acquiring examples of genuine Americana in order to preserve our past. Two, because Red Wing products combine beauty and utility, they are ideal for helping to achieve the popular "country" look in decorating one's home. Three, due to the fact that Red Wing clay products are no longer produced and continue to increase in value, collecting them has been and should continue to be a wise investment. The fourth reason is all encompassing. Because literally hundreds of types and styles of items were produced first by the stoneware companies and then by Red Wing Potteries, the variety alone provides the key ingredient to make collecting Red Wing an enjoyable hobby for anyone.

Americana

With the celebration of America's bicentennial as a nation in 1976, a renewed awareness of our rich heritage and an appreciation for those items which are uniquely American have re-emphasized the need for preserving that past. Understanding the lifestyle of our ancestors has come not only through books but also through the collecting and the displaying of items which characterized that lifestyle. Collectors have, and should, become "custodians of treasures" in order to allow future generations to experience the lives of our ancestors but without the hardships.

Red Wing stoneware products afford the collector not only tangible mementos of our ingenious past but also fascinating views of life without plumbing or electricity. The dreary routine of our ancestors' everyday lives was made more tolerable through the use of common and ordinary utilitarian objects which had been transformed into things of beauty. Hand decorated cobalt designs applied to well formed and beautifully glazed stoneware products provided our ancestors with functional works of art--"folk art" by our standards, but beautiful none the less.

The charming, yet primitive, bird design adorning this 20 gal. hand thrown salt glaze crock reflects the unpretentious integrity of American craftsmen from a bygone era.

Even after the time consuming hand decorating ceased, the beauty of Red Wing products continued in their graceful shapes and decorative glazes. Whether the pieces were hand turned or molded, the potters of Red Wing took pride in their ability to transform the most mundane household objects into works of art.

The beautiful, yet functional, spittoon, chamber pot, flower pot, wash bowl and pitcher and jugs shown here show that each piece was thoughtfully conceived and carefully executed.

Decorating Appeal

A casual glance through any household magazine will readily reveal that decorating with primitives, in general, and stoneware, specifically, is very much the growing trend. Red Wing stoneware can be used as decorative accents, as focal points when displaying collections or for a useful purpose since it is as functional as it is pleasing. Decorating with Red Wing stoneware is not only fun but also doubly pleasing since it enriches one's home and increases in value at the same time.

An assemblage of stacked salt glaze crocks makes a beautiful statement in any room. Here they are displayed in a bedroom. The glass cover added to the 20 gal. birchleaf crock converts it into an ideal bedside stand.

These Red Wing pieces form a decorative display in a family room setting. They are used with other primitives in order to provide a delightful blend of the old with just a touch of the new.

An ingenious mixture of period furniture, graniteware, kitchen utensils, general store items and Red Wing stoneware combines to add country charm to this kitchen setting.

Antique kitchen cupboards provide innumerable display possibilities for a stoneware collection--on, in, above and/or below. Creative utilization of space was as important in kitchens of the past as it is today.

This walnut pie safe is set off by a beautiful blue/white Red Wing lily bowl and pitcher displayed in combination with other unusual primitives.

Attractive examples of Red Wing stoneware, similar in size and color, are grouped here on an old wagon seat with a coverlet adding emphasis.

RWCS convention commemoratives (1977-1982) are highlighted here in an old pine medicine cabinet.

This fall floral arrangement in a Red Wing stoneware vase would provide a dramatic accent in any decor--antique or modern.

Beauty and utility come together in this decorative fireplace setting. The 20 gal. crock is a perfect container for firewood storage. The earth tones of the other primitive items add to the feeling of warmth.

Personal Pleasure and/or Investment Opportunities

While no investment can be called fool-proof and no item is ever guaranteed to increase in value, most Red Wing stoneware has shown a strong appreciation in value during the last five years. Like other antiques and collectibles, the supply of Red Wing is limited; however, many pieces are still available and, better yet, affordable. This combination of factors suggests that there is no better time to buy than the present.

For a collector, the primary rule of thumb when buying is to buy only those pieces that have personal appeal. By pleasing one's self, the buyer can give his collections its own personality. Then, if its value increases, that's a bonus.

There are, however, general factors to be considered before making a purchase whether for personal pleasure or for investment.

1. QUALITY--For the investor, quality is an invisible label indicating maximum worth no matter how rare the piece. Condition is only one component of quality. For the collector it is sometimes necessary to buy pieces with some damage until they can be upgraded at a later date. The condition of a piece is not as important with a rare item as it might be with a more common item. Workmanship and distinctive characteristics such as shape, decoration and glaze are additional ingredients that contribute to a piece of high quality.

2. COMPANY SIGNATURES--The importance of buying signed pieces cannot be overstated. For example, an unsigned miniature fancy jug can generally be purchased for under $25.00. The value of a similar jug signed on the bottom can be worth ten times that amount. Sidewall company stamps on salt glaze pieces more than double their value--everything else being equal. Bear in mind, however, that not all lines produced were signed. This in no way detracts from their value. Old catalogs and dump finds provide the proof necessary for company authenticity.

3. SIZE--For many collectors, fine pieces in miniature form hold a special fascination thereby increasing value. At the other end of the spectrum, the largest sizes of most product lines command higher prices as well.

4. RARITY--Again, many factors blend together in order for a piece to achieve a "rare" distinction. Scarcity is certainly one attribute. Pieces that are literally one of a kind will bring (and have brought) top dollar. Supply alone, however, does not guarantee a high price--nor does age. Spongeband pieces and pantry jars made

14

in the 1930's command much higher prices than some older and scarcer white or brown pieces made in the late 1800's. Supply, too, for particular pieces may be less in some geographic areas than others, increasing the demand and the price.

5. DESIRABILITY--The one over-riding factor, therefore, that dictates demand is group popularity. Beauty, eye appeal, decorating possibilities and personal taste very often determine the selling price of a particular piece.

Value Guide

Due to the arbitrary nature of the desirability factor described above (what's "in" this year may not be the next), a definitive value for any particular piece does not exist. The accompanying prices given in this book, therefore, are guides only intended to help a buyer determine an approximate measure of value. They represent the combined input and experience of many collectors, dealers and/or investors of Red Wing stoneware.

Many readers may have purchased some of the same items illustrated for much less or for much more. Keep in mind that **all** of the aforementioned factors must be taken into consideration, and, in the final analysis, the value of a particular piece is worth only what a particular buyer is willing to pay--considering desirability and affordability. Because of differing interests, what's too much for one collector may seem cheap to another.

The best advice we can offer a new collector is to learn all you can about your collecting interest. Read, communicate with other collectors, visit shops, shows, flea markets etc. to compare prices and to determine relative value in your area. Also, proceed with caution at auctions. Often, too much emotion and not enough reason are involved in the prices realized. The main thing is to have fun in the search, be open to new friendships with fellow collectors and enjoy your collection.

The range of value given here assumes that the piece is in mint condition even though the item illustrated may not be. For each item pictured, we have tried to give size (where applicable); bottom marking (refer to markings section--Chapter IV); and price--in that order. e.g. 1 gal. (M 4) $50.00-75.00. Bear in mind that certain pieces (particularly white shoulder jugs under 3 gal. in size and butter crocks) may display bottom markings other than those indicated on the pieces pictured. Likewise, bottom markings in addition to those shown in Chapter IV were used by the companies, but they were either similar to the ones we have chosen to identify or used too infrequently. Since most markings were proportionate in size to the pieces on which they appeared, they may not always look exactly the same in each case.

A glossary is also included in Chapter IV to help in identifying unfamiliar terms.

CHAPTER II: Product Lines

This chapter illustrates examples of major product lines. We have divided it into two categories: General Stoneware and Kitchen Stoneware. These categories are further divided into the various lines relating to each.

General Stoneware: Jugs

Advertised as "Our Specialty: Finely Glazed Jugs" and "The Celebrated Red Wing Jugs" this product line was one of the most prolific. In one catalog, alone, jugs were available in ten different shapes and, for each of them, there were many different sizes. The liquor trade probably provided the major market for jugs, although they were advertised as containers for "perfume," "syrup," "tomatoes or fruit," "druggist supplies," vinegar, etc. The many examples found by collectors today testify to their popularity.

Jug Styles

1. **"common"**--any jug that does **not** have a "crock" bottom; most are "beehive" in shape (e.g. bottom left)
2. **"shoulder"**--any jug that **has** a "crock" bottom; many variations of tops were molded to these bottoms; 6 examples are shown on page 20--standard, cone, ball, dome, pear and funnel. (e.g. bottom right)

Jugs

SALT GLAZE LEAF, BEEHIVE. Any decorated salt glaze beehive jug is rare, but for one to display a handsome leaf and to be side wall stamped as well is nearly unheard of. This 5 gal. beauty is just such a jug. (RW 1) $1,000.00-1,300.00; (unsigned) $250.00-300.00.

SALT GLAZE, " DOUBLE P", BEEHIVE. This hand turned, hand decorated 4 gal. beehive jug is the only one known to exist signed in this manner. (M 1) $1,000.00-1,300.00; (unsigned) $250.00-300.00.

SALT GLAZE "COMMON" JUG.
Another very rare, signed jug is this 1
gal. molded Minn. example. It is one of
the earliest molded pieces produced. (M
3) $200.00-250.00; (unsigned)
$30.00-40.00.

NORTH STAR SALT GLAZE JUG.
This 2 gal. all salt glaze jug with
"turkey eye" drippings is stunning. All
NS shoulder jugs have this "pear"
shaped top but most other tops are
glazed brown. (NS 1) $500.00-600.00.

SALT GLAZE "SHOULDER" JUG STYLES. Illustrated here are the six different styles of 1 gal. brown and salt glaze "shoulder" jugs. Left to right: 1. Standard top (RW 6) $100.00-125.00; 2. Cone top (RW 3) $125.00-175.00; 3. Ball top (RW 3) $150.00-200.00; 4. Dome top (M 3) $50.00-75.00; 5. Pear top (NS 1) $125.00-150.00; 6. Funnel top (M 2) $60.00-80.00.

SALT GLAZE "SHOULDER" JUGS. These are complete sets of RW cone top and NS pear top salt glaze jugs. Both are ca. 1894-1896. One half and 2 gal. sizes are difficult to find in any salt glaze jug style. Left to right: 1. 2 gal. (RW 4) $225.00-275.00; 2. ½ gal. (RW 3) $250.00-300.00; 3. 1 gal. (RW 3) $125.00-175.00; 4. 1 gal. (NS 1) $125.00-150.00; 5. ½ gal. (NS 1) $250.00-300.00; 6. 2 gal. (NS 1) $250.00-350.00.

SALT GLAZE SHOULDER JUGS. Shown here are complete sets of funnel top and dome top Minn. jugs. Left to right: 1. 2 gal. (M 2) $100.00-125.00; 2. ½ gal. (M 5) $100.00-125.00; 3. 1 gal. (M 2) $60.00-80.00; 4. 1 gal. (M 3) $50.00-75.00; 5. ½ gal. (M 5) $100.00-125.00; 6. 2 gal. (M 2) $100.00-125.00.

BALL TOP RW JUG. Notice the difference in shapes between this jug and the Minn. dome tops above. This jug is extremely difficult to find. 1 gal. (RW 3) $150.00-200.00.

NS WIDE MOUTH JUG. Wide mouth jugs were also referred to as "tomato or fruit" jugs. This is the only signed NS example we know of. 1 gal. (NS 1) $250.00-300.00.

BROWN BEEHIVE JUGS. These two Albany slip, hand turned beehive jugs have the number "5" etched into their glazes. They are some of the most beautiful examples of stoneware jugs and are the largest Albany slip glazed pieces made. Left to right: (RW 1) $500.00-600.00; (handle stamped RW 11) $500.00-600.00.

BROWN MINN. BEEHIVE. Known to be one of a kind, this 2 gal. early, hand turned jug is side wall stamped. (M 1) sold at auction 1982. $625.00.

BROWN MOLDED RW JUG. Another never before seen jug is this side wall stamped 1 gal. Notice the uniquely shaped neck. (RW 11) $400.00-500.00.

22

MOLDED "BIRD" JUGS. Each jug in this complete set of RW Albany slip jugs is seamed in the middle. Many of these include a stylized "bird" on their bottom markings. Left to right: 1. 2 gal. (RW 2) $150.00-175.00; 2. 1 gal. (RW 2) $75.00-125.00; 3. ½ gal. (RW 2) $125.00-150.00.

MINN. "COMMON" BROWN JUGS. Two styles of Minn., Albany slip molded jugs are represented here. Notice the difference in the neck styles. These jugs are seamed at the bottom. Left to right: 1. 1 gal. (M 2) $40.00-50.00; 2. ½ gal. (M 5) $35.00-45.00; 3. 1 qt. (M 5) $60.00-70.00; 4. ½ gal. (M 5) $45.00-60.00; 5. 1 gal. (M 2) $75.00-85.00.

NS "COMMON" JUG. This 1 gal. Albany slip NS jug is especially unique due to its stenciled company name decoration. It is a real prize. (NS 4) $800.00-1,000.00.

NS "COMMON" JUGS. Shown here is a complete set of Albany slip NS jugs. The two on the left are molded at the bottom and the one on the right is molded in the middle. ca. 1895. Left to right: 1. 1 gal. (NS 4) $150.00-175.00; 2. ½ gal. (NS 4) $125.00-150.00; 3. 1 qt. (NS 4) $150.00-175.00.

RW BROWN CONE TOP. This cone top RW jug style is typically found with a salt glazed bottom. Perhaps this was an experimental piece--unusual none the less. 2 gal. (RW 4) $400.00-450.00.

MINN. MOLDED BROWN JUG. Here is another atypical jug. It is a 1 gal. Albany slip jug that is usually found with a bail handle. This special handle was applied instead. 1 gal. (M 3) $175.00-225.00.

BROWN MOLDED JUGS. The beautiful 2 gal. Albany slip Minn. jug on the left was probably meant to be one of the first "fancy" jugs. It is, however, the only one known. The ½ gal. RW jug on the right has not been found in any other size. Left to right: 1. 2 gal. (M 2) $300.00-350.00; 2. ½ gal. (RW 6) $50.00-75.00.

MINN. WIDE MOUTH JUGS. These two "tomato or fruit" jugs are, again, molded at the bottom. Left to right: 1. ½ gal. (M 3) $35.00-55.00; 2. 1 gal. (M 4) $40.00-60.00.

WHITE MINN. STANDARD SHOULDER JUGS. Note the two different styles of qts. in this complete set of Minn. shoulder jugs. They all have "standard" tops. Left to right: 1. 2 gal. (M 12) $35.00-50.00; 2. 1 qt. (M 8) $60.00-80.00; 3. 1 gal. (M 12) $20.00-30.00; 4. ½ gal. (M 13) $20.00-30.00; 5. short 1 qt. (M 9) $100.00-150.00.

RW WHITE STANDARD SHOULDER JUGS. This set of RW white glaze shoulder jugs is similar indeed to the Minn. set shown above. Left to right: 1. 2 gal. (RW 4) $35.00-50.00; 2. 1 gal. (RW 8) $25.00-35.00; 3. ½ gal. (RW 11) $25.00-45.00; 4. 1 qt. (RW 7) $60.00-80.00.

RW WHITE CONE TOP JUGS. There evidently was a large market for white jugs in the late 1890's and early 1900's so many different shapes and sizes were produced. Left to right: 1. ½ gal. (RW 6) $70.00-90.00; 2. 1 gal. (RW 6) $40.00-60.00; 3. 2 gal. (RW 4) $30.00-50.00.

WHITE MINN. JUGS. Three jugs of differing shapes (funnel, dome and cone top) are shown here in white glaze. Left to right: 1. 2 gal. (M 2) $50.00-75.00; 2. 1 gal. (M 2) $50.00-75.00; 3. 2 gal. (m 12) $30.00-50.00.

WHITE JUGS. Pictured here are three additional styles of jugs in white glaze. The middle 1 gal. jug is more commonly found in brown glaze. Left to right: 1. ½ gal. (M 12) $30.00-50.00; 2. 1 gal. (M 2) $40.00-60.00; 3. ½ gal. (RW 8) $35.00-50.00.

WHITE MINN. "COMMON" JUGS. Again, jugs of this shape are infrequently found in white. Left to right: 1. 1 gal. (M 4) $50.00-75.00; 2. ½ gal. (M 5) $30.00-50.00.

WHITE WIDE MOUTH JUGS. The two jugs with the middle mold seams came in white glaze only. The 1 gal. jug on the right can also be found in brown. Left to right: 1. 1 qt. (RW 10) $35.00-45.00; 2. ½ gal. (M 12) $40.00-60.00; 3. 1 gal. (M 4) $50.00-70.00.

STANDARD TOP, WIDE MOUTH JUG. Here is a hard to find style of wide mouth shoulder jug. 1 gal. (M 9) $50.00-75.00.

SYRUP JUGS. These jugs are identified by their pour spouts. Left to right: 1. 1 gal. (M 12) $40.00-60.00; 2. ½ gal. (M 13) $40.00-60.00.

CONE TOP SYRUP JUGS. The cone tops on these jugs indicate an earlier production period than the standard top ones above. Syrup jugs in any style are not easy to find. Left to right: 1. 1 gal. (M 9) $50.00-70.00; 2. ½ gal. (M 9) $50.00-70.00.

15 GAL. BEEHIVE JUG. A turn of the century Union catalog advertised "10, 15 and 20 gal. jugs made to order. Stenciled for signs when desired." We are fortunate indeed that someone had this 15 gal. beauty commissioned in the first place and even more fortunate because it survives today. Sold at auction 1981 $2,650.00.

"ELEPHANT EAR" BEEHIVE JUG. The beauty of this hand turned 5 gal. white glaze jug is enhanced by the large "elephant ear" leaves which are so prominently displayed. Union oval $300.00-350.00.

BIRCHLEAF BEEHIVE JUGS. Not only is it difficult to accumulate a complete set of hand turned white glaze beehive jugs, but it is even more difficult to find them displaying both birchleaves and the Union oval. Left to right: 1. 3 gal. $140.00-160.00; 2. 4 gal. $225.00-275.00; 3. 5 gal. $140.00-160.00.

WING BEEHIVE JUGS. Shown here is another rare, and later, set of beehive jugs--each emblazoned with a red wing and an oval. Left to right: 1. 3 gal. $150.00-175.00; 2. 4 gal. $225.00-275.00; 3. 5 gal. $150.00-175.00.

UNUSUAL BEEHIVE JUGS. Four gal. jugs are hard to find in any style. These are even more unique because the left one is missing the oval and the right one has the oval upside down and does not have leaves or a red wing. Left $225.00-275.00; Right $175.00-225.00.

BIRCHLEAF BEEHIVE THRESHING JUG. This hand turned 5 gal. white glaze beehive is called a "threshing" jug. The hole near the bottom is for a wooden spigot making it easy to use while doing field work. No examples of this jug style can be found in any of the catalogs. $300.00-350.00.

WING BEEHIVE THRESHING JUG. Pictured here is another 5 gal. threshing jug with a spigot hole. This later example is marked with the large red wing and a RWUSCo oval. $350.00-400.00.

BIRCHLEAF SHOULDER JUGS. All bottom signed, these birchleaf shoulder jugs make a neat set. They date from approximately 1900-1906 and are molded rather than hand turned. Left to right: 1. 3 gal. (M 10) $75.00-100.00; 2. 4 gal. (M 10) $100.00-150.00; 3. 5 gal. (RW 9) $75.00-125.00.

WING SHOULDER JUGS. Each jug in this complete set of white molded shoulder jugs is marked with a wing and a RWUSCo oval. The 3 gal. is bottom marked as well. Left to right: 1. 3 gal. (RWU 1) $40.00-60.00; 2. 4 gal. $50.00-75.00; 3. 5 gal. $40.00-60.00.

BROWN TOP WING JUGS. Brown topped shoulder jugs displaying red wings only are very desirable. They were produced as late as the 1930's. Left to right: 1. 2 gal. $250.00-300.00; 2. 1 gal. $125.00-$175.00; 3. ½ gal. $125.00-175.00.

A brown topped shoulder jug displaying a red wing in a size larger than 2 gallons is rare indeed. 5 gal. $250.00-275.00.

The demand for fancy jugs exhibiting red wings far exceeds the supply. 2 gal. $350.00-400.00.

"FANCY" JUGS. Older than the "fancy" jug with the wing shown on the previous page, this jug style dates to the turn of the century. This complete set shows all eight sizes produced. Their contrasting glazes made them ideally suited for advertising purposes. Both Minn. and RW markings can be found.

2 gal. (RW 8) $200.00-250.00
1 gal. (RW 8) $125.00-175.00
½ gal. (RW 8) $150.00-200.00
1 qt. (RW 10) $75.00-100.00*
1 pt. (unsigned) $25.00-50.00; (if signed)
   $300.00-350.00**
½ pt. (RW 9) $150.00-175.00*
¼ pt. (M 10) $175.00-225.00*
1/8 pt. (M 10) $175.00-225.00*

*most common mark for this particular size
**difficult to find with any marking

BLUE BANDED JUGS. The 1 gal. jugs shown here are unusual not only for their attractive glazing but also for their strange "unattached" handle styles. They have been found with both Minn. and RW bottom markings. The 1 qt. shoulder jug in the middle is even more rare than the two cone tops. Left to right: 1. (RW 8) $375.00-425.00; 2. 1 qt. (M 8) $350.00-400.00; 3. 1 gal. (M 9) $325.00-375.00.

BLUE BANDED FANCY JUG. This wonderfully strange "cutie" is the only one known to exist. It is one pt. in size and, better yet, it is signed! 1 pt. (M 10) $500.00-600.00.

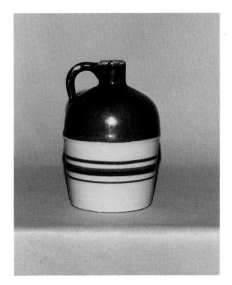

Bailed Jugs

BROWN BAILED JUG. This beautifully shaped and glazed 1 gal. bailed jug is the oldest style made by a RW stoneware company. It dates to the mid 1890's. 1 gal. (RW 6) $175.00-225.00.

BROWN MINN. BAILED JUGS. These three bottom marked Albany slip bailed jugs show two different styles. Any brown glazed bailed jug is rare. Left to right: 1. 1 gal. (M 3) $100.00-150.00; 2. ½ gal. (M 5) $100.00-150.00; 3. 1 gal. (M 2) $125.00-175.00.

RW WHITE BAILED JUGS. This set of white bailed jugs represents four different styles. The one on the left is the oldest (ca. 1895) and the one on the right is the newest (ca. 1930). Left to right: 1. 1 gal. (RW 6) $100.00-150.00; 2. ½ gal. (RW 6) $75.00-100.00; 3. 1 gal. (RW 7) $60.00-85.00; 4. 1 qt. (RW 10) $100.00-125.00; 5. 1 gal. (RWU 1) $75.00-100.00.

MINN. WHITE BAILED JUGS. These six Minn. bailed jugs again illustrate the three different sizes that were available for most styles. Also, examples of ½ and 1 gal. wide mouths, which are harder to find, are shown. Left to right: 1. 1 qt. (M 5) $100.00-125.00; 2. 1 gal. (M 6) $125.00-175.00; 3. ½ gal. (M 5) $75.00-100.00; 4. 1 gal. (M 12) $100.00-125.00; 5. ½ gal. (M 12) $75.00-100.00; 6. 1 gal. (M 12) $75.00-100.00.

BLUE MOTTLED BAILED JUGS. The "creme de la creme" of jug glazing is illustrated on these two 1 gal. bailed jugs. Though the jugs were molded, the sponging was applied by hand; thus, the patterns were not uniform. Both bottom signed, these jugs are very desirable and rare as well. Both, 1 gal. (M 12) $500.00-600.00 each.

Crocks

Crocks were made by the thousands and served as necessities for life in early America. The designs used for decorating early Red Wing salt glaze crocks carried on the tradition of American folk art.

SALT GLAZE "LILY" CROCK. The lily design first appeared in an 1894 Red Wing catalog and came in 12, 15, 20, and 30 gal. sizes. Stenciled words read, "MADE BY THE RED WING STONEWARE CO. RED WING, MINNESOTA." This stenciling on any item is rare. 30 gal. (RW 1) $800.00-1,000.00.

SALT GLAZE "BUTTERFLY" CROCK. The detail and artistry on this crock are excellent. Again, note the hard to find stenciling and a side wall Red Wing stamp as well. The similarity of the "30's" on these two crocks indicates that the same artist/potter made both pieces. Wow! 30 gal. (RW 1) $700.00-900.00.

SALT GLAZE "BUTTERFLY" CROCKS. The butterfly on the 30 gal. is huge--it measures almost 10" across. This is a fine collection by any standard--especially since they are all signed. Top, 20 gal. (RW 1) $300.00-350.00; 30 gal. (RW 1) $350.00-450.00; Bottom, both 10 gallons (RW 1) $275.00-325.00 each; (unsigned) $150.00-200.00.

SALT GLAZE "LEAVES" CROCK. A 40 gal. salt glaze crock is not supposed to exist. No where in the Red Wing literature is a crock this size advertised in salt glaze. Although not signed, there is no doubt as to its maker. $250.00-300.00.

LEAVES. This is an extremely fine example of a signed Minnesota 25 gal. crock. (M 1) $300.00-350.00; (unsigned) $150.00-200.00.

45

SALT GLAZE LEAF. The large and beautiful single leaf design makes this Minnesota crock an attractive addition to any collection. 10 gal. (M 1) $250.00-300.00; (unsigned) $100.00-125.00.

RW SALT GLAZE CROCK ASSORTMENT. These crocks are all side wall stamped and are fine examples of various designs used for decoration. Left to right: 1. butterfly (RW 1) $250.00-300.00; 2. leaf (RW 11) $225.00-275.00; 3. "P" (RW 1) $200.00-250.00; (unsigned) $75.00-125.00 each.

SALT GLAZE DOUBLE "P". Manufactured and signed by the Minnesota Stoneware Co., this design is sometimes called a "rib cage". 4 gal. (M 1) $250.00-300.00.

SALT GLAZE "P". The double side wall RW stamp makes this crock especially unusual. 6 gal. (RW 1) Sold at auction 1981 $350.00.

SALT GLAZE DOUBLE "P". An outstanding mark on the front adds to the beauty of this piece. 3 gal. (M 1) $250.00-300.00; (unsigned) $60.00-80.00.

SALT GLAZE CROCKS. These two 3 gal. crocks are both signed. The "drop 8" is not a commonly found design. The more common leaf is clean and neat. Left to right: 1. "drop 8" (RW 1) $225.00-275.00; 2. leaf (M 2) $200.00-225.00; (unsigned) $75.00-100.00 each.

SALT GLAZE CROCKS. (assortment of signed 2 gal. crock design styles). Left to right: 1. double "P" (M 2) $75.00-100.00; 2. target (RW 6) $100.00-125.00; 3. lazy 8 and target (M 2) $75.00-100.00; (unsigned) $50.00-75.00 each.

WHITE TRANSITIONAL CROCKS. This is a fine example of the "new" white glaze with the design and numbers still hand drawn. $150.00-175.00.

The double set of leaves on this transitional piece was applied with a stamp, but the gallonage was hand written. $175.00-200.00.

The use of stamps saved time in the production process and meant less dependence on the artistic skills of workers. $125.00-150.00.

MINN. OVALS. Crocks with a Minn. oval are very difficult to find. Most ovals have RW or Union Stoneware Co. printing. This crock has the leaves applied sideways making it a unique piece. 2 gal. $300.00-350.00.

STYLIZED "MSWCo". This Minn. marking is nearly impossible to find on any stoneware piece. Therefore, this is a great find. $350.00-400.00.

"ELEPHANT EAR" CROCKS. This set of crocks is neatly stacked for display. 2-6 gal. sizes can be found with Minn. bottom marks. "Elephant ears" and birchleaves were used interchangeably in a 1900 catalog illustrating the first white glazed crocks. 2-8 gal. $30.00-60.00; 10-15 gal. $60.00-80.00; 20 gal. $125.00-175.00.

WING CROCKS. The more familiar red wing decorates these newer crocks. Wings became the standard RWUSCo trademark sometime after 1906 and before 1909--perhaps to highlight the company name change. A 1909 dated post card showing wing crocks in a factory photo verifies this dating. 2-8 gal. $30.00-60.00; 10-25 gal. $60.00-80.00; 30-40 gal. $100.00-150.00; 50-60 gal. $250.00-300.00.

BIRCHLEAF CROCKS. Birchleaves were the only designs shown on crocks in a 1906 RWUSCo catalog. They were, however, phased out sometime before 1909. These two are also bottom marked. (both) (M 10) 2-8 gal. $30.00-50.00; 10-25 gal. $50.00-75.00; 30-40 gal. $75.00-125.00; 50-60 gal. $200-250.00.

1 GAL. WING CROCK. One gal. crocks were seldom decorated--and then only with a single red wing. Needless to say, they are in great demand. $275.00-325.00.

Churns

Churns have always held a fascination for stoneware collectors. The graceful curvature of the shapes are very pleasing to the eye. Many of the same designs used on salt glaze crocks were also used for churn decorations. Originally, they came in 2-8 gal. sizes with the 10 gal. added about 1896. The old salt glaze churns with Red Wing or Minn. company signatures stamped into the side walls are quite rare.

MOLDED "PARROT" CHURN. This salt glaze churn is truly magnificent. Most salt glaze churns were hand turned instead of molded. A Minn. bottom mark adds to this churn's rarity. 3 gal. (M 2) Sold for "over $2,600" in 1984.

MOLDED LEAF CHURN. This churn is from the same mold as the "parrot" and has the same bottom marking. 3 gal. (M 2) $500.00-600.00.

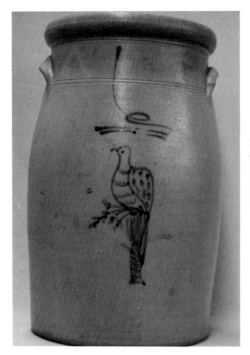

BIRD CHURN. Although not signed, the characteristics of this churn leads us to believe that it is a RW product. A similar churn--5 gal.--sold for $1,050 in 1981.

8 GAL. LEAF CHURN. A beautiful double leaf decoration adorns this uncommonly large churn. (unsigned) $275.00-325.00.

SIGNED RW CHURNS. This is the only signed butterfly churn known. The leaf on the 5 gal. churn is done in true folk art fashion. Both pieces are unusual and desirable. 1. butterfly (RW 1) $600.00-700.00; 2. leaf (RW 1) $500.00-600.00; (unsigned) $150.00-250.00 each.

Two more signed churns illustrate the beauty of cobalt markings on salt glazed clay. Note how the "4" blends into the leaf. 1. leaf (RW 1) $500.00-600.00; 2. "P" (RW 1) $450.00-550.00; (unsigned) $150.00-200.00 each.

MOLDED "ELEPHANT EAR" CHURN. Unusual blue "elephant ear" leaves and the unique Minn. oval combine to make this bottom signed Minn. churn very rare. 3 gal. (M 2) $400.00-500.00.

10 GAL. BIRCHLEAF CHURN. Churns of this magnitude are few and far between making this one a real gem. $400.00-475.00.

2 GAL. CHURNS. The wing churn on the left is unusual not only because there is no oval but also because it has earred handles unlike other wing churns. It is a perfect mate for the birchleaf churn on the right which displays an old style RWUSCo oval. $150.00-175.00 each.

WING CHURNS. Wing churns in sets are hard to match for beauty--especially when used to decorate a fireplace hearth. 2 gal. $150.00-175.00; 3 and 4 gal. $125.00-150.00.

5 AND 6 GAL. WING CHURNS. Churns in 3, 4 and 5 gal. sizes appear to be the most commonly found. 5 gal. $125.00-150.00; 6 gal. $150.00-175.00.

8 AND 10 GAL. CHURNS. The ridges caused by the hand turning process in making these two churns add to their beauty. 8 gal. $325.00-375.00; 10 gal. $400.00-475.00.

Water Coolers

Water coolers were production items from early in the stoneware companies' histories well into the RW Pottery era (after 1936). Salt glaze coolers are especially hard to find and, therefore, very valuable--particularly if they are signed. They are also among the most desired of all RW stoneware pieces.

RED WING SALT GLAZE "ICE WATER". The hand printed "Ice Water" and the detailed flower design add to the uniqueness and rarity of this cooler. (RW 1) $2,500.00-3,000.00.

RED WING BUTTERFLY. The price paid for this water cooler reflects its rarity and desirability. (RW 1) $1,400.00-1,600.00.

RED WING BUTTERFLY. Another style of butterfly decorates this well-formed water cooler. Butterfly designs similar to both of these appear on crocks and a few churns as well. 6 gal. (RW 1) $1,400.00-1,600.00.

RED WING DAISY WATER COOLERS. The beauty of these "daisy" designs is in their very simplicity. 4, 6 and 8 gal. (RW 1) $1,200.00-1,400.00 each.

RED WING DOUBLE LEAVES.
Leaves served as decorative designs on
many Red Wing items though few rival
these in beauty. 5 gal. (RW 1)
$1,400.00-1,600.00; (unsigned)
$350.00-400.00.

RED WING DOUBLE LEAVES.
Shape, glaze, decoration and size all
contribute to the elegance of this piece.
4 gal. (RW 1) $1,400.00-1,600.00; (un-
signed) $350.00-400.00.

DROP "8". This cooler is unusual not only for its attractive design but also because of its crock shape. 5 gal. (unsigned) $200.00-250.00.

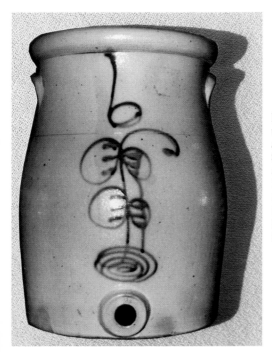

DOUBLE "RIB CAGE". Again unsigned, this water cooler can be attributed to the Minnesota Stoneware Co. due to its design and the round spigot hole. An 1895 Minn. catalog shows a water cooler with a similar "slug" shape. 6 gal. Signed (M 1) $1,500.00-1,700.00 (unsigned) $350.00-400.00.

BIRCHLEAF COOLERS. When white glaze replaced salt glaze, many of the old shapes were retained though stamps were used to speed the decorating process. The Ice Waters represented here are fine examples of the early white ware coolers. $275.00-325.00 each.

25 GAL. ICE WATER. The tremendous size and abundant decoration on this crock cooler make it very unique. $175.00-225.00.

WING ICE WATER COOLERS. These four coolers each display the "new" Red Wing Union trademark--the red wing. Top, 3 and 4 gal. $275.00-325.00 each; Bottom, 5 and 6 gal. $250.00-300.00 each.

TRANSITION COOLER. This rare 8 gal. cooler is certainly an odd one. The slug hole indicates a transition from the early salt glaze to the more modern style water cooler. 8 gal. $300.00-375.00.

ADDITIONAL WATER COOLER STYLES. Water coolers went through one more style change (left) before culminating in the style shown on the right in the 1920's. The gallonage number on the left hand cooler is found on the inside bottom. Two gallon coolers in these styles are the most difficult to find and range in price from $700.00-800.00. 5 gal. (most common size) $250.00-300.00 each with original lid.

Success Filters

Success filters were advertised in either a four gal. "family" size or a 10 gal. "hotel" size. Water in the upper crock would be "cleaned" as it moved through a filtering stone placed over a drip tube. The drip tube extended from the upper crock into the lower crock. Some filters also came with a stoneware base which enabled the spigot to be raised so that a cup could fit underneath.

 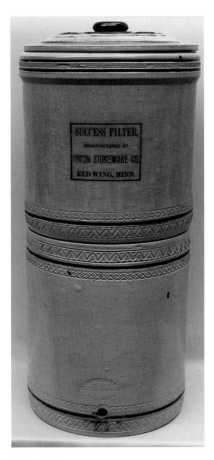

RED WING SALT GLAZE. The stenciling on the upper portion of this filter adds to the beauty of this piece. It reads "Success Filter, Natural Tripoli Stone, Patented July 7/89, Made By, The Red Wing Stoneware Co. Red Wing Minnesota." 4 gal. $650.00-850.00.

MINNESOTA SALT GLAZE. Pictured here is Minnesota's version of the Success Filter. The incised design on the clay differs from its RW counterpart as does the location of the blue bands. 4 gal. $650.00-850.00.

WHITE FILTERS. There are numerous variations of designs used on success filters. It can be a real challenge to try to match tops and bottoms. 4 gal. $250.00-300.00 each (complete with lid).

FILTER BOTTOMS. Two additional designs are represented on these filter bottoms. $75.00-100.00 each.

Spittoons

Although the function of spittoons is far from glamorous, their various shapes and glazes can be extremely beautiful making them very collectible. The multitude of incised designs found on the "German" spittoons can be matched with those used to decorate success filters.

MINNESOTA SALT GLAZE "GERMAN". This bottom signed Minn. spittoon is a true collector's item, as it appears to be the only one known. (M 2) $500.00-600.00.

TWO RED WING SALT GLAZE "GERMAN" SPITTOONS. With only slight variations, the designs on these spittoons parallel the decorative motif exhibited on the salt glaze RW success filter. (unsigned) $250.00-300.00.

MINN. BROWN SPITTOON. This dark brown bottom signed Minn. spittoon, again, is the only one known. Its diameter is just huge. (M 2) $400.00-500.00.

UNSIGNED SALT GLAZE. This spittoon appears in an old RW factory photo. $125.00-175.00.

RED WING SALT GLAZE. Because of its RW side wall stamp, this spittoon is rare indeed. (RW 1) $500.00-600.00.

WHITE "GERMAN" SPITTOONS. These three white spittoons all have different designs. Note the irregularities of the hand cut holes necessary for emptying the contents. (unsigned) $200.00-250.00 each.

BROWN/WHITE "CUSPIDORS". No, it's not a salesman's sample. Red Wing made the small one as a toy. It sold for 10¢. This style of spittoon was advertised as a "Fancy Spittoon." Left, Toy (unsigned) $200.00-250.00; Right, Minn. large spittoon (M 5) $275.00-325.00.

MOLD SEAM CUSPIDORS. Most collectors are unaware that spittoons of this shape (wide middle mold seam) were RW products. They appear in only one known catalog from the mid teens. Left, brown/white (unsigned) $80.00-100.00; Right, all brown (unsigned) $60.00-75.00.

B/W SPONGE. Still another spittoon shape is represented on this beautiful blue sponged spittoon. (unsigned) $200.00-250.00.

B/W MOLD SEAM CUSPIDORS. This gorgeous set of RW blue sponged spittoons represents all three sizes made (6, 8 and 10″ diameter across the top). The largest was for the "hotel" trade. They, too, have the wide mold seam and were never signed. Left to right: $300.00-350.00, $200.00-250.00, & $200.00-250.00.

Chambers and Combinettes

Chamber pots were vital necessities before indoor plumbing. Their shapes and decorations gave beauty to the most functional of all stoneware pieces.

BROWN CHAMBERS. All three stoneware companies made chambers. The glaze on this Minn. example is exceptionally beautiful. (M 5) $125.00-175.00.

Notice the fancier handle design on this RW chamber. (RW 6) $75.00-100.00.

BLUE BANDED CHAMBER. Though unsigned, the handle design is identical to the one on the brown Minn. chamber shown previously. This style also appears in RW advertising. $50.00-75.00.

This NS chamber with its original lid is a previously unknown item. Its characteristics are typically NS. (NS 4) $350.00-450.00.

WHITE CHAMBERS. These two signed RW chambers retain the "fancy" handles and represent both sizes produced (7 and 9″). The lid is believed to be original. Left, (RW 6) $60.00-85.00; Right, (RW 8) $60.00-85.00.

BROWN SPONGE COMBINETTE AND CHAMBER. Mottled combinettes and chambers first appeared in an early RW Union catalog. Again, they were probably never signed. $75.00-100.00 each.

BLUE SPONGE CHAMBER. Both styles were also made with a blue sponge motif. $150.00-200.00.

"LILY" COMBINETTE. This embossed lily decoration adds beauty to an otherwise plain piece. $150.00-200.00 (complete).

B/W EMBOSSED COMBINETTE. Though similar in shape and style to combinettes made by other non-RW stoneware companies, the pattern represented here is the only one shown in RW catalogs. $150.00-200.00 (complete).

Miscellaneous Household Stoneware

B/W HOT WATER BOTTLE WITH LEAF MOTIF. This hot water bottle, bottom signed, is exceptionally attractive and rare. (RWU 2) $550.00-650.00.

BROWN HOT WATER BOTTLES. Two different styles are shown here in brown. The leaf designed one was produced for a short time in the late teens and the triangular version appeared in the early 1920's. Left, (RWU 2) $125.00-150.00 (unsigned) $55.00-75.00; Right, (RWU 2) $175.00-225.00.

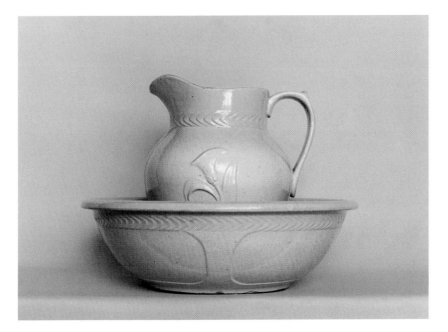

B/W LILY BOWL AND PITCHER. Shape, color and design combine to make this set an extraordinary example of RW artistry at its height. $400.00-500.00.

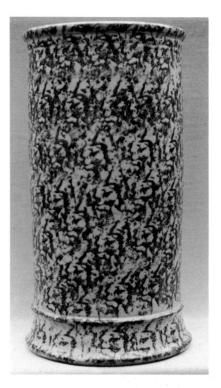

UMBRELLA STANDS. Umbrella stands are highly sought items. They are as useful today as they were in 1906 when they were first introduced. This all blue sponge example is stunning. (never signed) $550.00-650.00.

The red and blue sponging on this umbrella stand was applied in deliberate patterns. The glazing is nearly perfect. $500.00-600.00.

CHRISTMAS TREE HOLDER. A 1912 advertisement for this unusual piece boasted that "They will sell at sight. Everyone will want one if properly displayed as it eliminates all trouble in setting up tree." The tree was secured with either screws or wedges in the top holes. Later ones had a side hole through which water could be added--a strategic oversight. $300.00-350.00.

BROWN MINN. FLOWER POT. This beautiful and rare Albany slip flower pot is strikingly different from the bisque (unglazed) examples which are normally found. 7" (M 5) $175.00-225.00.

BISQUE FLOWER POTS AND SAUCERS. Flower pots and saucers were big sellers as they are advertised in every known catalog in one style or another. Furthermore, all three companies made them, though their designs varied. They came in sizes ranging from 2-12″. Pots, left to right: 1. (NS 4) $30.00-40.00; 2. (RW 6) $15.00-20.00; 3. (M 5) $20.00-25.00; Saucers, $10.00-15.00 each.

Kitchen Stoneware: Pitchers

The seemingly endless variety of shapes, glazes, decorations and functions has enhanced the desirability of stoneware pitchers even for non-Red Wing collectors.

RUSSIAN MILK PITCHERS. Though apparently never signed, the ½ and 1 gal. pitchers shown on the left with their graceful handles and shapes are Red Wing, and the ½ gal. pitcher on the right with its more rounded handle and straight-sided body appears in an 1895 Minn. Stoneware Co. catalog. $50.00-75.00 each.

PIPKINS. The three small pitchers shown here appear in only one of the known old catalogs--Union Stoneware Co. from 1896. They were either all brown or all white and came in four sizes (1-4 pints). Again, it is doubtful that they were ever signed. $50.00-75.00 each.

PIPKINS. This rare set of four pipkins illustrates the "newer" and more familiar brown and white style which first appeared in a turn of the century Union catalog. They, too, came in 1-4 pint sizes and, apparently, were discontinued in the mid teens. Left to right: 1. 1 pt. (M 10); 2, 3, 4 pt. (M 8) $175.00-225.00 each.

UNUSUAL PIPKINS. Two variations of the standard pipkin glaze are shown here. The Minn. bottom signed and mottled glazed one on the left is especially rare. Left, (M 10) $350.00-450.00; Right (unsigned) $50.00-75.00.

MUSTARD PITCHERS. One quart mustard pitchers were introduced in the 1896 Union catalog. Slight variations exist depending on which company produced them. The spout on the RW pitcher on the right is longer and more pointed than the Minn. version on the left. A brown and white signed Minn. example is also known to exist. Left to right: 1. (M 10) $60.00-80.00; 2. (RW 10) $60.00-80.00.

NORTH STAR MUSTARD PITCHER. North Star made their own version of the mustard pitcher. (NS 4) $175.00-225.00.

MOTTLED PITCHERS. First appearing after the formation of the RWUSCo, these pitchers were available in either blue or brown mottled glazes and in ¼ and ½ gal. sizes. RW sponge pitchers can be easily identified by the decorative knob on the handle top and the characteristic placement of the ridges. Blue, $150.00-200.00; Brown, $125.00-175.00.

MOTTLED PITCHER. The combination of blue and brown sponging on this pitcher makes it both rare and unusual. $300.00-400.00.

CHERRYBAND PITCHER. The earliest date known for this particular design is 1914 as evidenced on the all-white "Becker" advertising pitcher. Apparently this style was first produced as a special order item for Becker's use and then became a regular production item. It first appears in a catalog ca. 1916 which indicated three sizes and available in either blue or brown tint. Sharp mold markings and a shiny glaze add to this pitcher's value. $125.00-150.00.

BLUE AND WHITE PITCHER. Although unsigned and not known to appear in any RW publication, this pitcher was identified as a RW product by a pottery worker's descendant. It can be found in various sizes. The clay and glaze are very similar to the RW Dutch boy and girl pitchers. $70.00-90.00.

DUTCH BOY AND GIRL PITCHERS. These pitchers are testimony to RW's finest hour concerning pitcher production. However, they do not appear in any known RW literature. Because they are so similar in shape to the "Sleepy Eye" pitchers made by the Western Stoneware Co., one tends to believe that they were produced as a competing line. Their bottom mark indicates late 1920's--early 1930's production. (RWU 2) $450.00-550.00 each.

SPONGEBAND AND SAFFRON PITCHERS. Two other patterns introduced in the late 1920's and/or the 1930's were the spongeband and saffron lines. The earliest date known to appear on a spongeband advertising piece is 1929. Saffron ware came later using many of the same molds but made of more porous, yellowish clay. Pitchers in both lines came in the same two sizes and from the same molds. Top, Left to right: 1. (RWU 3) $125.00-150.00; 2. (RWU 3) $150.00-175.00; Bottom, Left to right: 1. (RWU 5) $60.00-85.00; 2. (RWU 5) $85.00-100.00.

SMALL DECORATIVE PITCHERS. Both of the small pitchers pictured here are unusual not only for their size and glazes but also for their bottom markings. The dark green matte glaze and the strange raised "Minn. S.W. Co" marking on the top pitcher are unlike anything else produced. The design of the bottom pitcher is a modified version of the top one. It is much lighter in weight. Top, $300.00-350.00; Bottom, (RWU 2) $300.00-350.00.

UNCOMMON PITCHERS. These two pitchers are made from the same molds as ones shown before but their glazes are yellowish/orange and bluish/green--again, probably experimental as they are the only ones known to exist. Top, $325.00-375.00; Bottom, $200.00-250.00.

TRANSPORTATION PITCHER AND MUGS. These specialty pieces were made for the 1933 World's Fair. The design represents the theme of the World's Fair--"A Century of Progress." Most known examples were finished with a white glaze; therefore, the blue and white glazed mug represents a stunning find. Top, Pitcher $125.00-175.00; Mugs $40.00-50.00 each; Bottom, Blue/white mug $65.00-85.00.

BARREL PITCHER. Many companies made barrel-shaped pitchers, although the RW design varies slightly from those produced by others. Hand drawn lines scratched into the glaze on the handle and spout add to their individuality. (RWU 3) $75.00-125.00; (unsigned) $35.00-50.00.

IRIS PITCHER. Among the last stoneware pitchers Red Wing made were those with embossed irises. They were made by Red Wing Potteries in the late 1930's or early 1940's. The mold design is quite similar to that of the Dutch boy and girl pitchers made at an earlier time. (RWP 1) $60.00-80.00.

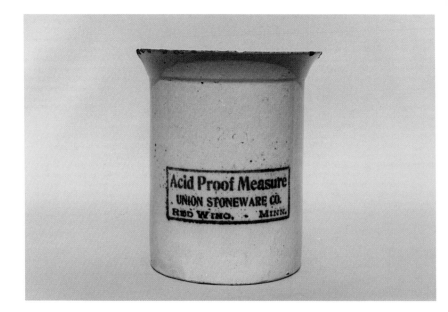

ACID PROOF PITCHER AND FUNNEL. One possible cause for the extreme rarity of marked Acid Proof Measure pitchers and funnels is that they appear in only one known catalog--indicating a short production period. The aforementioned catalog is an early RWUSCo publication dating them to about 1907. Why then do they display "Union Stoneware Co" on their logos? Pitcher $300.00-350.00; Funnel $350.00-400.00.

Bowls, Nappies, Cooking and Roasting Pans

Among the most common and numerous products the Red Wing companies produced were kitchen bowls and cooking containers. The early plain "milk pans" were supplemented in later years with all manner of various bowl glazes and designs. There was a never ending market for bowls of differing sizes as they were, and still are, a main stay in every household kitchen.

"Milk pans" appear in every stoneware catalog Red Wing ever published. Though their designs were identical, glazes and bottom markings vary. Before the "Union" in 1906 between Red Wing and Minn. Stoneware Companies, RWSCo was, by far, the biggest producer of bowls, as very few Minn. marked bowls exist.

MILK PANS. By size, the 7″ (illustrated here) and 10¾″ bowls are the most common. By color, brown and white RW bowls are easily found; signed blue milk pans are extremely difficult to find. Milk pans range in size from 4¾″ (½ pint) to 15½″ (3 gal.). Top row, both (M 11) $40.00-70.00 each; Bottom row, all (RW 11) Left to right: 1. beater bowl $15.00-25.00; 2. $75.00-125.00; 3. $20.00-40.00.

NORTH STAR MILK PANS. North Star made milk pans as well. Did they, themselves, produce the white one or was it made later from an old NS mold? The small one is very light as are many of the other small items made by North Star. All, (NS 4) $60.00-85.00 each.

SMALL SHOULDER BOWLS. Bowls of this shape do not appear in RW catalogs until after the 1906 Union. They came in two sizes, 1 pt. and 1 qt., and are not commonly found. Both, (RW 12) $35.00-60.00 each.

When the RW and Minn. Stoneware Companies joined forces in 1906, new lines and glazes began to appear--perhaps to meet the threat presented by the formation of the Western Stoneware Co. which occurred at the same time. One of the most conspicuous changes from the past was the introduction of mottled glazes. The paneled mixing bowls proved this new venture to be a success as they appeared in every catalog from 1906 into the 1930's. They were only available, however, in 6 sizes (6-11") until the 1930's when a 5" bowl was added. This is one very good reason for this size to be in scarce supply today.

PANELED SPONGE BOWLS. 5, 10, 11" sizes $75.00-125.00; others $50.00-75.00.

ALL BLUE SPONGE PANELED BOWL. $100.00-150.00 (rare).

ALL WHITE PANELED BOWL WITH BLUE BANDS. $50.00-75.00. (probably experimental).

GREEK KEY BOWLS. The Greek key "salad" bowls when first introduced in the mid teens came in only four sizes--6, 8, 10, 12" diameters. It wasn't until the 1920's that the odd sizes (7, 9, 11") were added. Again, this accounts for the fact that the odd sizes seem to be the hardest to find. 6-10" $50.00-75.00; 11 and 12" $75.00-100.00.

BROWN GREEK KEY BOWL. This brown oddity has an almost salt glaze appearance. $75.00-100.00.

The 1930's saw the inauguration of many new bowl designs and glazes. Most were never signed--the exceptions being some of the saffron lines and some bowls made by Red Wing Potteries. Most of the following bowls came in sizes ranging from 5-12″. Many of them were made from the same molds--only the glazes changed. The first four bowls shown are a case in point.

WHITE BOWL WITH BLUE BANDS. $40.00-60.00.

"RED" AND BLUE BANDED BOWL. $30.00-50.00 (has also been found in a 4″ size).

BLUE TINT BOWL WITH RED SPONGING. $60.00-80.00 (very unusual).

WHITE BOWL WITH RED AND BLUE SPONGING. $50.00-75.00.

The ridges on the following three bowls are narrower than those shown previously and reach almost to the bowls' rims.

SAFFRON BOWL WITH RED AND BLUE SPONGING. $45.00-65.00.

WHITE BOWL WITH RED AND BLUE SPONGING. (RWP 1) $50.00-75.00.

WHITE BOWL WITH BLUE BANDS. (RWP 1) $40.00-60.00.

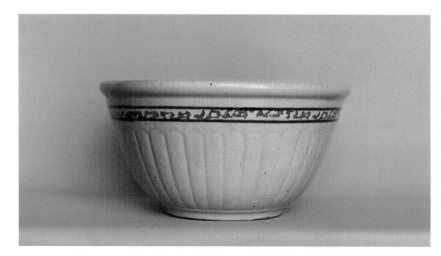

SPONGEBAND BOWL. This bowl design is a modified version of those just shown. The rim is much less pronounced, though the ridges are still there. They were available in nine sizes (4-12″). (RWU 3) 4, 5, 11, 12″ $100.00-150.00; others $65.00-90.00.

BLUE AND WHITE SHADED BOWL. The bowl and custard cup illustrated here share the same mold characteristics as the spongeband line, but they are not signed. Custard cup $40.00-50.00; Bowl $60.00-80.00.

BLUE BANDED MIXING BOWL. Various companies produced blue banded mixing bowls, but, again, those manufactured in Red Wing had a very distinctive shape. They too, date from about 1916 into the 1920's. Like the paneled sponge bowls, they originally came in only six sizes (6-11″) with the 5″ bowl added later. This design, in any size, is not easy to find. $35.00-55.00.

SAFFRON GRAPE BOWL. This saffron bowl has both a strange shape and an unknown grape pattern decoration. (RWU 5) $75.00-100.00.

Most "cap" bowls have two things in common: red and blue sponging and a 7″ diameter. Their shapes and mold markings vary, however.

CAP BOWLS--FULL PANEL AND RIDGES. 7″ with lid $75.00-125.00; 5″ $60.00-80.00. (rare).

CAP BOWL--SMOOTH SIDES. (RWU 4) $50.00-65.00.

CAP BOWL--CIRCLES AND LINES. With lid $125.00-175.00 (most unique).

CAP BOWL--SMOOTH SIDES WITH 3 HORIZONTAL lines. (RWU 4) $60.00-80.00.

Besides bowls, Red Wing also made a variety of casseroles or baking dishes. The only casserole examples to appear in any known Red Wing catalogs are the common all brown ones with bar handled lids and those in the spongeband design. They were available in four sizes. As you can see, from those two basic molds, other designs emerged.

CASSEROLE--ALL SPONGE. With lid $175.00-225.00 (very rare).

CASSEROLES--SPONGEBAND. With lids, (RWU 3) Smallest, $275.00-325.00; Others, $125.00-175.00.

CASSEROLE--SAFFRON. With lid (RWU 5) Smallest $100.00-150.00; Others $60.00-80.00.

CASSEROLES--WHITE WITH BLUE BANDS. Left to right: 1. (RWU 3) $75.00-100.00; 2. $35.00-50.00 (unsigned).

SPONGE BAKING DISH. Though this dish is not really a casserole (never had a lid), it was still used for baking. $75.00-100.00 (often display advertising, unsigned).

WHITE NAPPIES. Nappies or "pudding pans" appeared for the first time in a turn of the century Union catalog. They were available in 8, 9 and 10″ sizes--all white. Both companies made them though they are not easily found. Left to right: 1. (M 3) $60.00-85.00; 2. (RW 7) $60.00-85.00.

BLUE NAPPIES. Design and glaze changes for nappies or "baking pans" (later name) appeared after 1915. Sizes remained the same as did the "knotches" around the bottom rim. They came, however, at first in blue glaze only like the example on the right. Around 1920 the "blue tint" glaze replaced the dark blue. No signed examples are known. $60.00-80.00 each.

"Bailed cooking crocks or stew pans" were available in Red Wing stoneware catalogs from 1900 on. They were meant to be used on top of the stove; thus, their bottoms were flat for better heat distribution and they had wooden handles for lifting. Earliest examples were either unglazed on the outside or all brown. Later, they came in all white glaze. They did not have lids.

BAILED COOKING CROCKS. Left to right: 1. Bisque (RW 7) $100.00-125.00; 2. Brown (RW 7) $150.00-200.00; 3. White (RW 8) $75.00-100.00.

MEAT ROASTERS. Meat roasters were designed for oven use. They came with lids and their bails contained no wooden handles. They, too, had a long production life--from 1900 on with only slight design modifications. Bisque (M 7) $125.00-150.00.

Canning, Packing and Preserving Containers

Because freezers for long term storage were not available in the "pre-electric" time of our ancestors and glass containers were not yet in vogue for canning, stoneware jars of all shapes and sizes were household necessities.

SALT GLAZE JAR WITH STONE COVER. The tall, cylindrical shape of this salt glazed preserve jar is very unusual. This signed example with its original lid is the only one known. (M 5) $200.00-250.00.

RW BROWN PRESERVE JAR. This 1 gal. side wall stamped, Albany slip preserve jar is rare indeed. It, too, took a stoneware lid. (RW 11) $250.00-350.00.

RW PRESERVE/SNUFF JARS. "Preserve" and "Snuff" jars were very similar in shape and both came with stone covers. Snuff jars were advertised in ½-20 lb. sizes and preserve jars were advertised in ¼-2 gal. sizes with "larger sizes made to order". Left to right: 1. 4 gal. (RW 8) $125.00-150.00; 2. 2 gal. (RW 8) $100.00-125.00; 3. 1 gal. (RW 8) $35.00-55.00.

MINN. PRESERVE/SNUFF JARS. These are Minn. versions of the preserve and/or snuff jars. A 4 gal. size is also known to exist for this set. These came originally with salt glaze lids. Left to right: 1. 2 gal. (M 4) $100.00-125.00; 2. 1 gal. (M 5) $35.00-50.00; 3. ½ gal. (M 3) $35.00-50.00.

NORTH STAR PRESERVE/SNUFF JARS. North Star made their own line of these jars. Left to right: 1. 1 gal. (NS 2) $125.00-175.00; 2. ½ gal. (NS 2) $125.00-175.00.

WHITE PRESERVE/SNUFF JARS. Both Minn. and RW made preserve/snuff jars in white glaze as well as brown. Left to right: 1. 1 qt. (RW 10) $75.00-100.00; 2. ½ gal. (RW 11) $40.00-60.00; 3. 1 gal. (RW 8) $50.00-70.00; 4. 1 gal. (M 4) $50.00-70.00; 5. ½ gal. (M 3) $40.00-60.00; 6. 1 qt. (M 8) $75.00-100.00.

WAX SEALERS. These were the primary canning jars of yesteryear. Tin lids fit into the grooved tops and melted wax was poured around the edges for sealing; thus, the name "wax sealers." So far, only the barrel shaped quarts have been found with RW markings. Left to right: 1. 1 qt. (RW 3) $40.00-55.00; 2. ½ gal. (M 3) $30.00-40.00; 3. 1 gal. (M 5) $75.00-100.00; 4. ½ gal. (M 3) $30.00-40.00; 5. 1 qt. (M 5) $55.00-65.00.

NORTH STAR WAX SEALERS. Again, North Star had their own line of the same product. Left to right: 1. 1 gal. (NS 2) $175.00-225.00; 2. ½ gal. (NS 2) $175.00-225.00.

RED WING WAX SEALER. This straight sided qt. wax sealer is unique because of its shape and its raised RW bottom marking. It is the only known RW item to have this type of signature (see page 151). 1 qt. (RW 5) $125.00-175.00.

WHITE MINN. WAX SEALERS. Two white wax sealers are pictured here. Again, white examples are more difficult to find than brown ones. Here you see, as well, a tin lid and red sealing wax that were used with these jars. Left to right: 1. 1 gal. (M 5) $75.00-100.00; 2. ½ gal. (M 3) $50.00-70.00.

STONE MASONS. Stone Mason fruit jars came with either black or blue labels and most were patent dated Jan. 24, 1899. Left to right: 1. 1 gal. $275.00-325.00; 2. ½ gal. $125.00-150.00; 3. 1 qt. $125.00-150.00.

"MASON CAP" DOME TOP STONE JARS. RWUSCo was sued and was no longer able to use the word "Mason" as part of their jar logos. This newer shape and logo change (ca. 1916-1920) came right before glass jars dominated the market; hence, the reason for their scarcity. Left to right: 1. ½ gal. $550.00-650.00; 2. 1 qt. $600.00-700.00; 3. ½ gal. $600.00-700.00.

BAILED PACKING JARS. Advertised in 3, 5, 10 and 20 lb. sizes, this line enjoyed a long production life. Various RW and Minn. bottom markings can be found. They were used mainly for packing preserves, jams and fruit butters. Left to right: 1. 3 lb. (M 12) $60.00-80.00; 2. 5 lb. (M 9) $50.00-75.00; 3. 10 lb. (RW 7) $50.00-75.00; 4. 5 lb. (RW 11) $50.00-75.00.

BAILED PACKING JAR. Three and five gal. sizes with red wings were later additions to this line. With their stone covers, they make a great place for storing potatoes. 3 gal. $125.00-175.00.

SAFETY VALVE JARS. Some of these self-sealing jars display a May 21, 1896 pat. date which indicates that they were among the first white ware products. The line was discontinued around 1920. The middle jar above has the original hardware intact which is most unusual. The dot of red glaze on the lid was to be matched with the red dot on the lip of the jar to insure proper sealing. Left to right: 1. 1 gal. (RW 9) $125.00-150.00; 2. ½ gal. (M 8) $100.00-125.00; 3. 1 qt. (RW 11) $125.00-150.00; with original hardware, add $50.00.

BALL LOCK JARS. These self-sealing jars replaced the safety valve line. They came in 3 sizes (2, 3 and 5 gal.) and were continued into the 1930's as some display small wings. The 2 gal. size is usually seen with a brown top. $100-125.00 each. (large wing, complete).

5 GAL. PRESERVE JAR. This unusual jar is pictured in an old factory photo by the hundreds; but, today, this is the only one known marked in this fashion. $500.00-600.00.

KOVERWATES. These were placed inside of crocks in order to keep food submerged under the preserving liquid. Bottom and side holes let the brine come to the top. Pictured here are the 3, 4, 5, 10, 15 and 20 gal. sizes. They also came in 6 and 25 gal. sizes which are extremely hard to find. 3, 6 and 25 gal. $125.00-150.00; all others $75.00-100.00.

Bean Pots

RED WING BEAN POT. Pictured in an 1894 RWSCo catalog, this "Boston" bean pot style was available in three sizes (qt., ½ and 1 gal.). RWSCo bean pots are the most difficult to find. 1 gal. (RW 6) $125.00-175.00.

NORTH STAR BEAN POTS. Though similar in shape to their RW counterpart shown above, these North Star pots have shorter "necks." Left to right: 1. 1 gal. (NS 5) $75.00-125.00; 2. ½ gal. (NS 5) $75.00-125.00.

MINN. BEAN POTS. Here are two examples of the Minn. version of the "Boston" bean pot. Note the lack of stoneware handles and the straight sides. Left to right: 1. 1 gal. (M 2) $75.00-125.00; 2. ½ gal. (M 5) $75.00-125.00.

BEAN POT AND CUPS. Looking for all the world like a pipkin without a spout, this bean pot shape is pictured in a catalog ca. 1916. The four "individual bean pots" or custard cups represent all three companies and came in 6 and 9 oz. sizes. Left to right: 1. (NS 4) $75.00-100.00; 2. (M 10) $40.00-60.00; 3. ½ gal. pot (M 8) $100.00-125.00; 4. and 5. (RW 12) $25.00-40.00.

BROWN AND WHITE BAILED BEAN POTS. Pictured here are three later-styled, bailed, two-tone bean pots. They were originally advertised in the mid teens as being available in a pt. size as well, though no signed examples are known. Left to right: 1. 1 qt. (RWU 2) $50.00-75.00; 2. ½ gal. (RWU 2) $40.00-60.00; 3. 1 gal. (RWU 2) $40.00-60.00.

SAFFRON BEAN POTS. These two saffron bean pots represent the last bean pot shape made in Red Wing out of stoneware. Brown and white pots like these were introduced in the 1930's and are most often found displaying advertising logos. The red and blue sponge example shown here is extremely rare. Left to right: 1. 1 gal. saffron with band (RWU 5) $40.00-60.00; 2. 1 gal. sponge (RWU 5) $175.00-225.00 (with original lids).

Butter Crocks

SALT GLAZE "LOW" BUTTER JARS. Salt glaze butter crocks were made in three sizes--3, 5 and 10 lbs. although 3 lb. examples are not known. They came with or without "tie rings." Left to right: 1. 10 lb. (RW 4) $50.00-75.00; 2. 10 lb. (M 2) $50.00-75.00; 3. 5 lb. (M 5) $35.00-50.00.

NORTH STAR BROWN "LOW" BUTTER JAR. North Star also made butter crocks. All that have been found are in the 2 lb. size. Some are marked with just an indented star while others also include the full company signature on the bottom. 2 lb. (NS 5) $70.00-90.00; if full signature (NS 3) $200.00-250.00.

MINN. BROWN "LOW" BUTTER JARS. Butter jars were, evidently, popular items as they were available in so many sizes. Besides the ones shown, a 20 lb. size was also advertised. Many times, if you look closely, you can see the outline of the fingers that held the jars as they were "dunked" into the Albany slip. Left to right: 1. 10 lb. (M 2) $50.00-70.00; 2. 2 lb. (M 5) $30.00-40.00; 3. 5 lb. (M 5) $30.00-40.00; 4. 1 lb. (M 5) $60.00-80.00; 5. 3 lb. (M 5) $40.00-60.00.

RED WING BROWN "LOW" BUTTER JARS. These crocks are similar in shape to the Minn. examples above except for the 10 lb. size. The mold for it is like the salt glaze example shown previously. Again, the 3 lb. size is very difficult to find. Left to right: 1. 10 lb. (RW 4) $50.00-70.00; 2. 5 lb. (RW 4) $30.00-40.00; 3. 2 lb. (RW 7) $30.00-40.00; 4. 1 lb. (RW 6) $60.00-80.00.

BROWN MINN. "HIGH" BUTTER JARS. Any crocks which were 6 gal. in size or smaller were actually referred to first as "butter jars" and later as "high butter jars" in company advertisements. All three companies produced the qt. and ½ gal. sizes in brown, but only Minn. examples are known in the 1 gal. size. Left to right: 1. 1 gal. (M 3) $50.00-70.00; 2. ½ gal. (M 5) $30.00-40.00; 3. 1 qt. (M 5) $40.00-60.00.

BROWN NORTH STAR "HIGH" BUTTER JARS. Though small, these may be the only examples of NS "crocks" one can find. North Star was the only RW company to make the two smallest sizes. Left to right: 1. ½ gal., 1 qt., 1 pt. (NS 4) $100.00-125.00; ½ pt. (NS 4) $150.00-200.00.

MINN. WHITE "LOW" BUTTER JARS. It is nearly impossible to accumulate a complete, marked set of white butter jars as is shown here. Left to right: 1. 20 lb. (M 2) $250.00-300.00; 2. 3 lb. (M 12) $25.00-35.00; 3. 10 lb. (M 12) $30.00-40.00; 4. 2 lb. (M 5) $30.00-40.00; 5. 5 lb. (M 9) $25.00-35.00; 6. 1 lb. (M 5) $50.00-75.00.

RED WING WHITE "LOW" BUTTER JARS. Once again, the shapes of the 10 lb. examples differ depending on which company produced them. A 20 lb. size, though advertised, bottom marked RW has not been found. Left to right: 1. 10 lb. (RW 4) $30.00-40.00; 2. 2 lb. (RW 7) $30.00-40.00; 3. 5 lb. (RW 8) $25.00-35.00; 4. 1 lb. (RW 6) $50.00-75.00; 5. 3 lb. (RW 7) $30.00-40.00.

WHITE "HIGH" BUTTER JARS. Shown here are the three smallest sizes of tall butter crocks in white glaze. Again, both RW and Minn. Companies produced them. The qt. size is, by far, the most difficult size to find. Left to right: 1. 1 qal. (M 12) $20.00-35.00; 2. ½ gal. (M 5) $30.00-50.00; 3. 1 qt. (M 5) $70.00-90.00.

"ELEPHANT EAR" ODDITY. The open jar pictured here is an unusual size--it's a 2 gal. crock cut in half which makes it the same size as a 20 lb. butter crock. (M 2) $175.00-225.00.

MINN. 20 LB. BUTTER JAR. This unusual 20 lb. butter crock displays a hand written "20#" indicating very early white ware production. It also has a neat Minn. bottom mark. (M 2) $250.00-300.00; (if unsigned) $75.00-100.00.

20 LB. BUTTER JAR WITH RED WING. The deep blue lettering and the attractive red wing combine to make this later crock one of the most beautiful and, therefore, desirable pieces produced. $275.00-325.00.

TALL AND LOW BLUE SPONGE BUTTER CROCKS. These butter crocks prove, again, that everyday household objects can be beautiful as well as functional. They date from approximately 1906-1916 and came in various shapes and sizes. (never signed) $150.00-200.00 each.

BLUE/WHITE EMBOSSED BUTTER CROCKS. Long thought to be RW products, proof now exists confirming the authenticity for these stunning butter crocks. They appear in a RWUSCo advertisement (ca. 1916) in these three sizes and came with or without bail handles. The blue/white glaze and embossed floral design contribute to their extreme beauty. (never signed) $225.00-275.00 each with original lids.

Special Lines

SPONGEBAND (Gray Line). Introduced in the late 1920's this line of kitchenware was a popular seller then and remains highly popular among collectors today. It was, perhaps, intended as a competing line to Western Stoneware Company's Colonial kitchenware. The demand for spongeband pieces has, thus far, exceeded the supply; therefore, they command high prices. The items shown here are especially difficult to find.

STACKING REFRIGERATOR JARS. Three sizes (RWU 3) $325.00-375.00 each (with lids). CAKE STAND. (RWU 3) $800.00-900.00.

COOKIES. (RWU 3) $325.00-375.00 (with lid). REAMER. (RWU 3) $500.00-600.00. BATTER BOWL. (RWU 3) $300.00-350.00.

HANGING SALT BOX. (RWU 3) $500.00-600.00 (with lid). SHAKERS. $250.00-275.00 each.

MUGS. (RWU 3) $325.00-375.00 each.

PANTRY JARS. Another kitchen line that is enjoying great popularity among collectors of Red Wing stoneware is the graduated set of pantry jars. They were advertised as being available in seven sizes (3 lb.-4 gal.). In addition, a small 1 lb. jar was manufactured. Although never shown in RW literature, an 8 gal. pantry jar has surfaced as well.

Left to right: 1. 5 lb. (most common) $250.00-275.00; 2. 1 gal. $500.00-600.00; 3. 1 lb. $250.00-275.00; 4. 10 lb. $500.00-600.00; 5. 3 lb. $375.00-425.00 (with original lids).

Left to right: 2, 3, 4 gal. $850.00-1,100.00 each.

Miscellaneous Kitchen Ware

BAILED B/W REFRIGERATOR JARS. These jars were available in 3 and 5 lb. sizes. Food stored in them remained cold long after it was removed from the refrigerator. They were introduced around 1920. $125.00-150.00 each (with lids).

STACKING REFRIGERATOR JARS. These jars were made to stack on top of other jars of similar size in order to save refrigerator space. Notice the two different printing styles. $85.00-125.00 each.

BEATER JARS. These five beater jars from the 1930's were all made from the same mold design. Each pattern represented can be found on other pieces of kitchen stoneware. Left to right: 1. (RWP 1) $50.00-65.00; 2. (RWP 1) $50.00-75.00; 3. (RWP 1) $175.00-225.00; 4. (RWU 3) $125.00-150.00; 5. (RWU 5) $50.00-75.00.

PIE PLATES. Although both RW and Minn. Stoneware Companies made pie plates, they are difficult to find today. First shown in an 1896 catalog, they were available in a 9" size only. Left to right: 1. brown (RW 7) $100.00-125.00; 2. white (M 5) $85.00-100.00; 3. brown (M 3) $100.00-125.00; 4. salt/brown (M 3) $150.00-175.00.

CHAPTER III: Specializing

It seems that when one begins collecting Red Wing products, his goal is to acquire at least one of every item produced. He soon learns that because of lack of space in his house and/or availability of funds and hard to find pieces he has to limit his collecting. A possible solution to this common malady is to specialize. This decision, though seemingly restraining, provides, instead, other benefits. It is not only more economical and more rewarding but it also allows for the diversity of tastes and personalities and enables one to become an "expert" in a particular area.

Some possibilities which are open to Red Wing collectors are:

1. by decoration (e.g. hand drawn leaves)
2. by company (e.g. North Star products)
3. by product lines (e.g. churns, bailed jugs)
4. by sets (e.g. variety of shapes, sizes and glazes of same item)
5. by use (e.g. kitchenware)
6. by color (e.g. sponge, blue/white, brown)

Examples of each of the above specialty categories can be found in the previous chapter.

Two additional areas which are rapidly becoming favorites among collectors are miniatures and pieces displaying advertising.

Advertising

The stoneware companies of Red Wing offered an endless variety of items from which an enterprising and progressive businessman could choose to promote his business and or products. In fact, there were very few, if any, product lines that could not be used for this purpose--no matter how big or how small. Stoneware pieces displaying both advertising and the manufacturer's marking are highly prized by collectors.

This beautiful, signed salt glaze jug would be rare even without advertising; with advertising it is nearly one of a kind. 1 gal. (RW 6) $300.00-350.00.

Since stenciled advertising usually predated the more common stamping method, this 1 gal. cone top jug must have been one of the very earliest white glazed pieces made--dating it to the mid or late 1890's. 1 gal. (RW 6) $250.00-300.00.

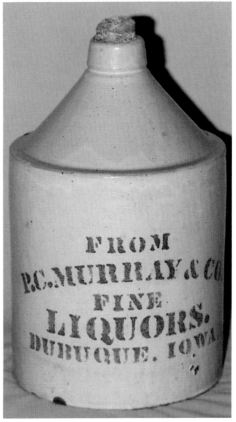

The contrasting brown and white glazes on these jugs made them ideally suited for advertising purposes. It would appear that this Chicago wine company's elaborate picture advertisement depicting Bacchus, god of wine, among the grapes takes the honors for creativity in advertising logos. Left to right: 1. ½ gal. shoulder, $75.00-100.00 (unsigned); 2. 1 gal. fancy, (RW 8) $275.00-325.00.

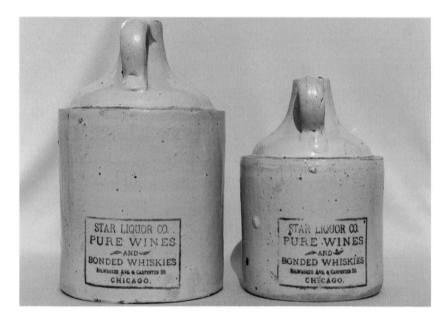

Reversing the location of the advertising on these jugs was intentional so that paper labels could be applied to the fronts. Both, (M 12) $100.00-150.00 each.

The Ewing, Nebraska business pro-
moted on this advertising churn
boasted of its "Dry-Goods, Clothing,
Shoes and Groceries." 4 gal.
$400.00-450.00.

Water coolers are not frequently found
with advertising. The "Sanitary School
Appliances" advertising on this old
style cooler reflects their popularity for
use in school houses. 8 gal.
$325.00-375.00.

The RWUSCo was commissioned by different companies, from time to time, to make certain one of a kind advertising wares for the purpose of promoting their businesses. This pitcher with an entirely new shape is an example of a "special order" item. The logo for this Hull, Iowa firm had to be placed on the inside bottom due to the all-over sponging. $325.00-375.00.

Another "special order" piece is this "Pitts Bros." storage jar. Though similar in design to regular pantry jars, the single top and bottom blue bands, unique lid and differing size make it special indeed. $300.00-350.00.

Both bottom signed, these bailed jugs are extremely rare--the 1 qt. one because of its fancy jug design and the ½ gal. one because of its beautiful blue sponging. Left to right: 1. (RW 10) $300.00-350.00; 2. (M 12) $600.00-700.00.

By far the most personal touch that advertising items afford the collector is to display the collector's name. Lucky are the people whose name is Peterson. Left to right: 1. butter crock $200.00-250.00; 2. pitcher $500.00-600.00; 3. mug $125.00-175.00; 4. bean pot $100.00-125.00.

Miniatures

People have always been attracted to those things that are smaller than their normal-sized counterparts. Capitalizing on this fascination for small items, the Red Wing companies produced many items in miniature form. These miniatures were usually given away as souvenirs for conventions or by commercial companies containing samples of their products for promotional purposes.

The examples above represent three different jug styles each commemorating conventions held in the city of Red Wing. Left to right: 1. 1929 State Elks Convention (RWU 3) $300.00-350.00; 2. 1915 Southern Minn. Medical Association Convention $500.00-600.00; 3. 1927 Improved Order of Redmen Convention $350.00-450.00.

"Souvenir of Red Wing" jugs might have been given away by the stoneware companies at the annual State Fair or sold by local merchants of the community. 1/8 pt. cone tops, $200.00-250.00; 1/8 pt. fancy $250.00-300.00.

"Souvenir of Excelsior Springs, Missouri" jugs were, more than likely, sold or given away with samples of their famous mineral water. The "1903" on the 1/8 pt. and pt. jugs help in establishing dating periods for brown and white fancy jugs. 1/8, ¼ and ½ pts. $225.00-275.00 (if signed); unsigned $100.00-125.00; 1 pt. $250.00-350.00 (if signed); unsigned 100.00-150.00.

The shiny brown glazes on these miniature jugs makes them especially unusual and attractive. They were, perhaps, not widely marketed due to their inability to be used for advertising. At any rate, they are very rare. Left to right: 1. ½ pt. (RW 9) $300.00-400.00; 2. 1/8 pt. $75.00-100.00 (unsigned).

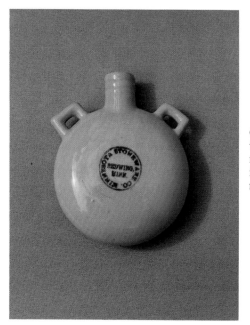

Canteens were made to commemorate the completion of the Red Wing Armory in 1901. The Minn. circle stamp is the only adornment on this unique miniature. $350.00-450.00.

Two different styles of traveling bags testify to the diversity of miniatures produced by the Stoneware Companies. The bag on the left was produced for the 1912 United Commercial Travelers' Convention and is a tiny bottle. "Souvenir of Red Wing" is stamped on the bottom of the bag on the right. Left: (RWU 2), $400.00-500.00 each.

CHAPTER IV: Reference Section

This chapter provides the reader and/or collector with information which should increase his knowledge of Red Wing stoneware; and, at the same time, increase the pleasure derived from his collecting mania.

Dates To Aid In Dating Particular Lines

1. 1878-1897--salt glaze and early brown ware
2. 1895--1st white ware introduced (small pieces)
3. 1897--salt glaze totally phased out
4. 1897-1906--"elephant ear" leaves and birchleaves used interchangeably to decorate crocks; use of Union oval began, though individual company bottom markings used as well.
5. 1906--mottled glazes introduced
6. 1906-1908--birchleaves used alone for decorating; 1st with Union oval and then with RWUSCo oval
7. 1908 or 1909--red wing 1st used as sole trademark decoration
8. 1915--wire handles on 4-30 gal. crocks patented
9. 1916 (approx.)--blue/white glaze 1st introduced
10. 1917--hand turning abandoned
11. 1947--stoneware production ceases altogether

Red Wing Collectors' Society

As a means for collectors to communicate, the Red Wing Collectors' Society was born in April 1977 with the publication of its first Newsletter. Its first convention was held in July 1977 in Red Wing. Membership has increased more than ten fold since that first year, and conventions continue to be held each July in Red Wing.

Benefits of Society membership include the Newsletter; educational opportunities; a medium of exchange for items and information; friendship; and the opportunity to purchase a Society commemorative piece each year. Originally priced from $4.00-10.00, they have continued to increase in value each succeeding year. Miniature salt glaze crocks from the first convention now command over $200.00 each. (see page 13)

Lids

An original lid displayed on a particular piece provides the crowning touch. They also add considerable value to any item, as they are quite rare since they were easily broken. Worth depends, in many cases, on a collector's need for a particular lid.

NORTH STAR SALT GLAZE LID. $50.00-75.00.

SMALL SALT GLAZE LID. Notice the tall "button" knob on this small flat lid. It could have been used on any early brown preserve or snuff jar or bean pot. $10.00-15.00.

SALT GLAZE CROCK LIDS WITH "PETALS". These RWSCo lids came in many sizes. The all salt glaze example was fired on the top layer in the kiln. $75.00-100.00 each.

WHITE CROCK LIDS. NS white lids most often appear in the 4 gal. size. "Button" petal lids are older than the "bar" handled ones which were introduced at the same time as bail handled crocks (1915-16). Left to right: 1. NS "button" lid $40.00-60.00; 2. RW "button" lid $50.00-70.00; 3. RW "bar" handled lid $40.00-60.00.

BAIL HANDLED LID. Lids for larger crocks came with bail handles for easier leverage. They are extremely heavy. RWUSCo $60.00-90.00 (depending on size).

MINN. CROCK LID. Minn. lids (salt glaze or white) with these modified "petals" are exceedingly rare. 4 gal. $75.00-100.00.

SMALL RW "BUTTON" LIDS. This assortment of white lids demonstrates the similarity of lids which came on snuff jars, preserve jars, Hazel butter or lard jars, bailed jars etc. Often they were interchangeable. $5.00-15.00 each.

BEAN POT LIDS. Again, the "button" lids predate the bar handled ones. $5.00-10.00 each.

RW BUTTER CROCK LIDS. These lid examples provide more proof that the small raised button knobs and bar handles were characteristic of RW lids. These were all produced after the 1906 Union and can provide verification of authenticity on unmarked pieces. $25.00-45.00 each.

PANTRY JAR LIDS. All pantry jar lids are identifiable due to the petals and set of double blue bands with the exception of the smallest two sizes. $75.00-125.00 each.

WATER COOLER LIDS. On bar handled water cooler lids, the gallonage number and "W" are incised in the petals. Water cooler lids are often found with a big chunk out of one side-- put there deliberately so that a dipper handle could rest over the edge of the cooler. $75.00-125.00.

OLD-STYLE BUTTON WATER COOLER LID. This style of cooler lid has the gallonage number and the "W" appearing on the "button" top. $75.00-125.00.

SPONGEBAND LIDS. The lid on the right is flat for stacking refrigerator jars. All other pieces had the petal lids as shown on the left. $50.00-85.00 each.

SAFFRON LIDS. Left: $20.00-30.00; Right: (see page 121) $40.00-50.00.

MISCELLANEOUS LIDS. Left: ovenware "cap" bowl $40.00-50.00; Right: B/W floral cannister $50.00-75.00.

CHURN LIDS. Red Wing churn lids can be recognized by their tapered shapes. $25.00-40.00 each.

BLACK SPONGE LID WITH PETALS. It is not known what this unusual lid matches. 1 gal. $50.00-75.00.

LARGE DARK BLUE SPONGE LID. An incised "10" on this lid indicates gallonage but not, however, whether it was for a crock, water cooler or something else. $50.00-75.00.

Red Wing Stoneware Co. 1877-1906

RW 1

RW 2

RW 3

RW4

RW 5

RW 6

RW 8

RW 7

RW 9

RW 10

RW 11

RW 12

Minnesota Stoneware Co. 1883-1906

M 1

M 4

M 2

M 5

M 3

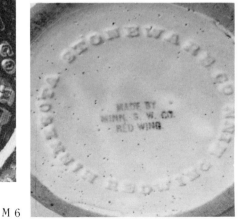

M 6

M 7

M 8

M 10

M 9

M 11

M 12

North Star Stoneware Co.
1892-1896

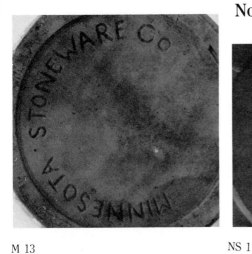

M 13

NS 1

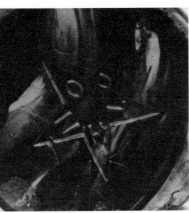

NS 2

NS 3

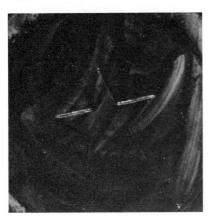

NS 4

NS 5

Red Wing Union Stoneware Co. 1906-1936

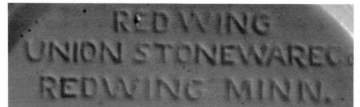

RWU 1

RWU 2

RWU 3

RWU 4

RWU 5

Red Wing Potteries
1936-1967

RWP 1

156

Glossary

A. Manufacturing Process:
 1. **hand turned**--stoneware shaped by hand from clay on a potter's wheel
 2. **molded**--stoneware made from clay which is pressed into a mold forming the desired (and standardized) shape
B. Glazes (colors):
 1. **salt glaze**--("tan" appearance)--stoneware put into kiln unglazed; salt shoveled into kiln during firing vaporizes and allows the compound sodium to form a shiny, yet transparent, natural glaze which acts as a sealant
 2. **Albany slip**--("brown" ware)--a particular type of clay when thinned with water forms opaque, brown glazes; shade of brown depends on amount of iron present in the clay and/or atmospheric variations in the kiln during firing; used as an interior glaze to prevent seepage or as an interior **and** exterior glaze on smaller pieces; pieces were either "dipped" into vat of slip glaze or the glaze was "poured" over the piece itself; "Albany slip" and "brown" are used interchangeably to describe color of glazes on pieces pictured in this book
 3. **white glaze**--(Bristol or zinc glaze)--opaque glaze made with large quantities of zinc oxide; the quality of Red Wing's white ware was outstanding--little or no crazing (glaze cracks)
 4. **bisque**--term used to denote the appearance of an unglazed item; e.g. flower pots
 5. **"turkey eye"** dripping--appears commonly on salt glaze pieces that were on top of stack during firing; globs of sodium collected on kiln bricks and dripped onto pieces below
 6. **mottled**--various colors sponged by hand onto white ware for decorative purposes; "red", "brown" and blue were most commonly sponged onto Red Wing stoneware
C. Markings and Decorations:
 1. **side wall stamped**--company name impressed into clay wall of piece with a metal stamp; found mostly on salt glaze items
 2. **oval**--later method of company identification; blue or black oval applied with a rubber stamp to white ware; "Union" oval used (approximately) 1897-1907; Red Wing Union Stoneware Co. oval used (approximately) 1907-1936
 3. **"bird" design**--design incised on the bottom of jugs of a certain style made by Red Wing Stoneware Co. which resembles a flying bird (pages 23 and 151)
 4. **coggle wheel** design--designs impressed into clay in circular arrangements done with a patterned wheel; used mostly on success filters and "German" spittoons
 5. hand applied **cobalt decorations**--used on salt glaze pieces; refer to salt glaze jugs, crocks, churns and water coolers in Chapter II for examples of the following most commonly used decorations: lily, butterfly, daisy, leaf, P, double P, drop 8, lazy 8 and target
D. Miscellaneous Terms:
 1. **tie ring**--a groove in the clay, or formed by ridges of clay, at the top of a crock or jug for string to rest while holding a cloth cover in place
 2. **"fancy"**--any piece that was dipped partially in brown glaze and partially in white glaze for a two-tone effect

Index

159

PRICE GUIDE

•JUGS•

Page

18 Leaf, Beehive-
(RW1) $1,200.00-1,400.00
(unsigned) $275.00-325.00
"Double P" Beehive-
(M 1) $1,200.00-1,400.00
(unsigned) $275.00-325.00
19 "Common" Jug-
(M 3) $225.00-275.00
(unsigned) $35.00-45.00
North Star Jug-
(NS 1) $550.00-650.00
20 "Shoulder" Jug Styles-
Standard Top $100.00-125.00
Cone Top $125.00-175.00
Ball Top $150.00-200.00
Dome Top.............. $50.00-75.00
Pear Top $125.00-150.00
Funnel Top $60.00-80.00
Cone & Pear Top-
2 gal. $225.00-275.00
½ gal. $250.00-300.00
1 gal. $125.00-175.00
1 gal. $125.00-150.00
½ gal $250.00-300.00
2 gal. $250.00-350.00
21 Funnel & Dome Top-
2 gal. $100.00-125.00
½ gal. $100.00-125.00
1 gal. $60.00-80.00
1 gal. $50.00-75.00
½ gal. $100.00-125.00
2 gal. $100.00-125.00
Ball Top RW Jug-
1 gal. $150.00-200.00
NS Wide Mouth Jug-
1 gal. $300.00-350.00
22 Brown Beehive Jugs-
(RW 1) $600.00-650.00
(RW 11) $600.00-650.00
Brown Minn. Beehive $625.00
Brown Molded Jug-
(RW 11) $450.00-550.00
23 Molded Bird Jugs-
2 gal. $150.00-175.00
1 gal. $75.00-125.00
½ gal. $125.00-150.00

Page

23 Minn. "Common" Brown Jugs-
1 gal. $40.00-50.00
½ gal. $35.00-45.00
1 qt. $60.00-70.00
½ gal. $45.00-60.00
1 gal. $75.00-85.00
24 NS "Common" Jug-
(NS 4) $1,000.00-1,200.00
NS "Common" Jugs-
1 gal. $150.00-175.00
½ gal. $125.00-150.00
1 qt. $150.00-175.00
25 RW Brown Cone Top-
2 gal. $400.00-450.00
Minn. Molded Brown Jug-
1 gal. $200.00-250.00
26 Brown Molded Jugs-
2 gal. $350.00-400.00
½ gal. $60.00-80.00
Minn. Wide Mouth Jugs-
½ gal. $35.00-55.00
1 gal. $40.00-60.00
27 White Minn. Shoulder Jugs-
2 gal. $35.00-50.00
1 qt. $60.00-80.00
1 gal. $20.00-30.00
½ gal. $20.00-30.00
Short 1 qt. $100.00-150.00
RW White Shoulder Jugs-
2 gal. $35.00-50.00
1 gal. $25.00-35.00
½ gal. $25.00-45.00
1 qt. $60.00-80.00
28 White Cone Top Jugs-
½ gal. $75.00-95.00
1 gal. $40.00-60.00
2 gal. $30.00-50.00
White Minn. Jugs-
2 gal. $50.00-75.00
1 gal. $50.00-75.00
2 gal. $30.00-50.00
29 White Jugs-½ gal. .. $40.00-60.00
1 gal. $40.00-60.00
½ gal. $40.00-55.00
White Minn. "Common" Jugs-
1 gal. $50.00-70.00

Schroeder's Antiques Price Guide

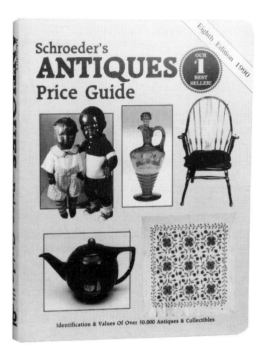

Schroeder's
ANTIQUES
Price Guide

OUR **1** *BEST SELLER!*

Eighth Edition 1990

Identification & Values Of Over 50,000 Antiques & Collectibles

Schroeder's Antiques Price Guide has climbed its way to the top in a field already supplied with several well-established publications! The word is out, *Schroeder's Price Guide* is the best buy at any price. Over 500 categories are covered, with more than 50,000 listings. From ABC Plates to Zsolnay, if it merits the interest of today's collector, you'll find it in Schroeder's. Each subject is represented with histories and background information. In addition, hundreds of sharp original photos are used each year to illustrate not only the rare and the unusual, but the everyday "fun-type" collectibles as well. All new copy and all new illustrations make Schroeder's THE price guide on antiques and collectibles. We have not and will not simply change prices in each new edition.

The writing and researching team is backed by a staff of more than seventy of Collector Books' finest authors, as well as a board of advisors made up of well-known antique authorities and the country's top dealers, all specialists in their fields. Prices are gathered over the entire year previous to publication, then each category is thoroughly checked. Only the best of the lot remains for publication. You'll find the new edition of *Schroeder's Antiques Price Guide* the one to buy for factual information and quality.

No dealer, collector or investor can afford not to own this book. It is available from your favorite bookseller or antiques dealer at the low price of $12.95. If you are unable to find this price guide in your area, it's available from Collector Books, P.O. Box 3009, Paducah, KY 42001 at $12.95 plus $2.00 for postage and handling.